The Life of
Little Nellie
of Holy God
1903-1908

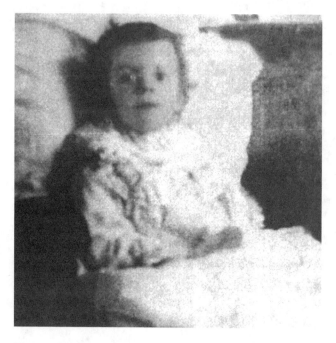

Photo of Little Nellie shortly before she died. Nellie is called "The Little Violet of the Blessed Sacrament."

The Life of Little Nellie of Holy God

1903-1908

THE LITTLE VIOLET OF THE BLESSED SACRAMENT

"Suffer the little children to come unto me, and forbid them not; for of such is the kingdom of God."
—Mark 10:14

TAN BOOKS AND PUBLISHERS

Imprimatur: Rev. Msgr. David D. Kagan, J.C.L.
               Vicar General
               Rockford, Illinois
               October 15, 2007

The Nihil Obstat and Imprimatur are official declarations that a book or pamphlet is free from doctrinal or moral error. No implication is contained therein that those who have granted the Nihil Obstat or Imprimatur agree with the contents, opinions or statements expressed.

Cover design by Sebrina Higdon.

ISBN: 978-0-89555-852-7

Printed and bound in the United States of America.

TAN BOOKS AND PUBLISHERS
2007

When Pope St. Pius X heard about Little Nellie of Holy God, he exclaimed, "There! That is the sign for which I was waiting." Soon afterward the Holy Father issued *Quam Singulari* (1910), allowing young children to receive Holy Communion.

(See page 90.)

"There will be saints among the children."

—Pope St. Pius X
(See page xiv.)

Publisher's Preface and Acknowledgments

Following our re-publication of the little picture book, *Little Nellie of Holy God* by Sister M. Dominic, R.G.S., illustrated by Sister John Vianney, S.S.N.D., we have sought to bring together the best available materials on Nellie in order to make known the rest of her story.

Three main sources have been used in this compilation. Earnest efforts have been made to select the best elements of each in order to present the precious facts about Nellie but eliminate excessive commentary.

Perhaps the earliest of these three main sources is a small book entitled *Little Nellie of Holy God: Story of the Life of a Saintly Irish Child,* by A Priest of the Diocese of Cork, "Printed by Guy & Co. Ltd.," 70, Patrick Street, Cork, 1912 and/or 1915. We were informed by Sister Imelda O'Driscoll, R.G.S. of the Good Shepherd Sisters of Sunday's Well, Cork, who sent us a copy of this rare book, that this priest was Rev. Dean Scannell, who had known Nellie personally and who was present at the exhumation of her body. Rev. Scannell was the dean of the diocese and secretary of the Bishop. He is also called Dr. Scannell, Rev. Dr. Scannell, and Monsignor Joseph Augustine Scannell. His book bore an Imprimatur from T. A. O'Callaghan, *Ord. Praed., Episcopus Corcagienis* [Bishop of Cork]. Sister Imelda, who stated "We hold the sole copyright," gave us permission to reprint this book, and the current Provincial Leader of the Good Shepherd Sisters in Ireland has given us permission to use material from Msgr. Scannell's book in the present compilation.

We quote here the Preface from Msgr. Scannell's book to establish the reliability of his work:

"I have been asked [by the Bishop of Cork, Dr. T. A. O'Callahan, O.P.] to write this story of the life of 'Little Nellie of Holy God.' I have interpreted as a command the expression of a wish coming from such a quarter. Besides, I shall always treasure the memory of the day on which I met that saintly child.

"The case of little Nellie has reached that stage when enthusiasm must be held in check by prudence, and when theory, however devotional, must yield to a calm consideration of the facts. Accordingly, some short time ago, those who had lived in closest intimacy with little Nellie were invited to state, clearly and concisely, their recollections of that brief life. A number of attestations were forwarded to Rome, with the assurance that everything therein contained could, if necessary, be testified on oath. Those documents were translated by a Roman priest, Don Ugo Descuffi, and arranged in a brochure entitled: *Nellie Organ— Cenni Biografici.* By express permission of the Holy Father, the little book was dedicated to His Holiness Pope Pius X.

"The same documents have been placed at my disposal together with some additional information, for the accuracy of which I have received a similar guarantee.

"In view of possible criticism, I wish to draw attention to a point of considerable importance. Owing to her delicate health—little Nellie was an invalid from the day of her admission to the Convent School at Sunday's Well—the person most in contact with the child was the Resident Nurse. Miss Hall was then a recent convert to Catholicity; she had read very little Catholic literature, and was still under instruction. Consequently the contention that little Nellie's extraordinary ideas and sayings were all inspired by her Nurse seems to refute itself.

"My task has not been a very arduous one, and I shall feel amply rewarded if this pamphlet should, in any slight degree, conduce to a greater devotion to Our Divine Lord in the Most Holy Sacrament of His Love."

Another main source was the small book by Margaret Gibbons entitled *Little Nellie of Holy God,* bearing a Foreword by Most Rev. John Gregory Murray, Archbishop of St. Paul, published by The Newman Press, Westminster, Maryland, in 1949. This book bears an Imprimatur from Most Reverend Francis P. Keough, D.D., Archbishop of Baltimore, October 29, 1948. In his Foreword (1948), Archbishop Murray notes that Little Nellie's story has a special interest for American readers because "Mother Francis," the Reverend Mother of the Convent where Nellie lived, had been for the preceding 15 years the Mother Provincial of the Convent of the Good Shepherd in St. Paul, Minnesota. The Archbishop also mentioned the "miracles of grace" which "occur daily in every House of the Good Shepherd throughout the world."

We quote here Miss Gibbons' Author's Foreword:

"Nothing that appears in the following pages is set down from hearsay. Every detail has been confirmed to the writer in personal interviews with the nun who was Nellie's Reverend Mother in 1907-08, as well as with two other Sisters who knew the child intimately.*

---

* "These interviews took place during July, 1928, but I am writing now from their written record. The interviews with Mary Long were in August, 1934—also recorded and confirmed."
                                        —Margaret Gibbons' footnote.

"Mary Long, too, who had charge of Little Nellie during the same period, kindly granted many and repeated interviews. There are also the Reverend Dr. Scannell's attested facts.

"The informants mentioned, let it be said, cover in their statements practically all the matter contained in the sworn depositions forwarded to Rome within two years of Nellie's death, which took place in Sunday's Well, Cork, February 2, 1908."

Margaret Gibbons' book includes a Preface by the above-mentioned Mother Mary of St. Francis Xavier—Nellie's "Mudder Prancis." In this Preface (1948), Mother Francis states:

"I was Superior of the Convent of the Good Shepherd at Sunday's Well during Nellie's brief lifetime and can confirm all the author narrates within the pages that follow. I knew Miss Gibbons personally and spent many pleasant hours with her, rehearsing the doings and sayings of this child of destiny. She gave unstintingly of her time and energy to make this book possible, and the clients of Little Nellie will be forever grateful to her, and Nellie herself will not be unmindful of her in Heaven."

Mother Francis herself passed to her reward in 1960 at the age of 99. She died at the Good Shepherd Home in St. Paul, Minnesota.

The third main source for the present book was an anonymous, undated stapled booklet entitled *Little Nellie*, which began with the words, "William Organ, Nellie's father," and which was sent to us with permission for reprint by Sister Imelda O'Driscoll, R.G.S. of the Good Shepherd Sisters of Sunday's Well, Cork, Ireland. The current Provincial Leader of the Good Shepherd Sisters in Ireland has given us permission to use material from this booklet in the present compilation.

Two of these three main sources rendered many of Nellie's words in baby-talk spellings (though not with complete consistency among the sources). We have kept many of these spellings but in some cases have used normal English spellings instead, for a smoother-flowing text.

It is from the third-mentioned source, the booklet entitled *Little Nellie,* that a number of the illustrations in the present book have come. A few additional pictures were graciously supplied to us by Leo Madigan, founder and director of Fatima-Ophel Publishing House, Fatima, Portugal, which publishes Mr. Madigan's own book entitled *Princesses of the Kingdom: Jacinta Marto and Nellie Organ.* Among the images supplied by Mr. Madigan are two from a collection of 18 drawings of events in Little Nellie's life. The photographic plates of these drawings had turned up in a London auction house in approximately the 1970s and were bought by an Irishman who recognized their subject as Little Nellie. Mr. Madigan is in touch with the current owner of the plates (Gus Nugent of Clonmel, Co. Tipperary), but Mr. Madigan says that "efforts to trace the artist have always drawn a blank." It is thought that the images were probably published in Père Roncés' French biography of Little Nellie (see footnote on p. 91); the 18 images also appear in Leo Madigan's *Princesses of the Kingdom*.

We are much indebted and very grateful to the Good Shepherd Sisters—both for recording their precious memories of Little Nellie and for sending us materials and giving us clearance to publish them. Special thanks to Sister Noreen O'Shea, R.G.S. and to Sister Helen Anne Sand, R.G.S. It seems that Providence has directed these materials on Little Nellie into our hands, and we are happy to be able to gather together the various elements of her story and pass them on.

It is gratifying to note that the great Fr. Reginald Garrigou-Lagrange, O.P. (1877-1964) knew of and esteemed Little Nellie of Holy God. Treating of the growth of Sanctifying Grace in the soul, he wrote:

"An interesting point in this connection is that which Pope Pius X had in mind when, in prescribing an earlier age for First Communion, he said: 'There will be saints among the children.' These words seem to have found their fulfillment in the very special graces which have been granted to several children, taken very early into heaven, who are today proving to be the source of so many vocations to the priestly and the religious life: such as little Nelly [sic], Anne de Guigné, Guy de Fontgalland, Marie-Gabrielle, T. Guglielmina and several others in France and Belgium—souls that remind us of the Blessed Imelda, who died of love while making her thanksgiving after her First Communion. Our Lord, who said: 'Suffer the little children to come unto me,' is able evidently to endow these souls with great sanctity at a very early age; He sows the divine seed in greater or less abundance in souls, according to His good pleasure. (See Collection *Parvuli,* Lethielleux, Paris.)"*

The old Convent of the Good Shepherd Sisters was sold in 1993, and then it burned down in 2003. However, there is still a small Good Shepherd community at the same location. The old convent cemetery is still in place, and Nellie's

---

* Fr. Reginald Garrigou-Lagrange, O.P., *The Three Conversions in the Spiritual Life* (formerly *The Three Ways of the Spiritual Life*) (London: Burns Oates & Washbourne, 1938; Rockford, Illinois: TAN, 2002), p. 80, n.1.

grave can still be visited—though not without some difficulty, at present, for safety reasons since the fire. Sunday's Well is centrally located in the city of Cork. We are advised that the best way to get there is by taxi and that the taxi driver should be directed to the Good Shepherd Sisters' current convent, since access to the cemetery is best through their property (the former gate-house). If the gate to the graveyard area is locked, the Sisters can unlock it.

We understand that the Nellie memorabilia— her shoes, her bed, her rogue tooth, her toys—are now in the possession of Mr. Michael Murphy of Cork. These items were displayed at the Dungarvan Museum, County Waterford in August of 2003 to commemorate the centenary of Nellie's birth. People arrived from all over Ireland to view the exhibit, which had to be extended for several weeks. The museum's curator stated that the visitors to the Nellie Organ exhibit outnumbered the visitors in the museum's entire prior history.

Pope St. Pius X gave his opinion that Nellie was in Heaven, referring in a letter to "Nellie, who was called to Heaven while still a little child." (See page 94). The Holy Father asked for and obtained a relic of Little Nellie. When asked about the possibility of canonizing her, he responded that God must manifest His Will by miracles.

(See p. 92.) The Pontiff also endorsed Nellie as a model for young communicants. (See p. 93). These words and deeds of the saintly Pius X, himself now canonized, would seem to give the "green light" for Catholics to pray to Little Nellie and to ask for her intercession.

—The Publishers
February 22, 2007

Contents

The Life of
Little Nellie
of Holy God
1903-1908

ᴖ *Chapter 1* ᴖ

Nellie's Family

WILLIAM ORGAN, Nellie's father, was married to Mary Aherne on July 4, 1896, in the village of Portlaw, Co. Waterford, Ireland. The Sisters of Mercy said of Mary when she was at school there: "She was a light-hearted, innocent girl, full of fun and frolic, but generous, straightforward and devout." William told his sister, a Sister of Mercy: "It was Mary's piety that won me."

William Organ said of his own family: "The branch to which I belong had been settled for generations in and around Dungarvan. I may say they were very humble Catholic folks, whose sole inheritance was that sterling Faith which has survived the centuries of Ireland's bitter sorrow.

"Mary Aherne, Nellie's mother, a native of Portlaw, Co. Waterford, like me, her husband, came of a humble Catholic family poor in world's wealth, but rich in those gifts of Heaven for the lack of which no boon on earth can compensate."

There in Portlaw the Organs lived for just one

year. Then, with dread conditions of unemployment facing them, William Organ had to choose between emigration and enlistment as a soldier. He chose the latter. In October, 1897, he joined the British Army, then in occupation in Ireland, and a garrison of which had long been established in the maritime town of Waterford.

The marriage was blessed with four children: Thomas, David, Mary and, lastly, Nellie, who was born on August 24, 1903, in the "married quarters" of the Royal Infantry Barracks.

Soon afterward, perhaps the next day, she was brought to the parish Church of the Trinity ("Trinity Without"), where the precious little soul was regenerated in the saving waters of Baptism.* She received the name of "Ellen," though she would be familiarly called "Nellie."

"When only two," Nellie's father writes, "she would clasp my hand and toddle off to Mass, prattling all the way about Holy God. That was the way she always spoke of God, and I do not know where she could have learned it." Nellie loved her father dearly, and her first request when her mother went out was to buy a rosary for Daddy. One night her father said he was going on sen-

---

* An article on the website of Waterford County Museum states that Nellie was baptized "in the Old Ballybricken Church." Apparently this was an alternate name for the same parish church. The quaint name "Trinity Without" must refer to the church's location *outside of,* or *without,* some boundary line.

tinel duty. Nellie said, "I will be sentinel in your place."

"You go to sleep," said her father.

"No," said Nellie, "I shall wait for you"—and when he returned some hours later she was awake, waiting for him.

The holy names were the first words that Nellie learned, and at night the family Rosary was said. Her mother taught her to kiss the crucifix and the large beads, a habit which Nellie retained.

In 1905 the family moved to Spike, an island-fort situated in Cork Harbor. The mother's health, which had never been robust, now visibly declined.

Mrs. Organ, always pious, turned in her last months entirely to God, and her rosary was never out of her hands. Toward the end she clung to Nellie with such transports of affection that the child had to be torn, almost rudely, from her dying embrace. She died of consumption, or tuberculosis, in January, 1907.

Little Nellie, not yet four years old, followed the remains of her holy Irish mother to its lowly resting place. Afterwards, it was always as "my dead Mudder" that Nellie spoke of her.

The eldest of the Organ children was only nine at the time. The father had to be engaged all day long in military duties, so a neighbor, with calls from her own home to be attended to, gave occasional help in the Organ household. This makeshift arrangement, however, was a poor one, and, on top of it all, Nellie was painfully delicate and seemed to require special care.

The truth is that she had a crooked spine, though this was not recognized till she came into the care of the Good Shepherd Sisters. The trouble had begun at the time when Nellie was a very small baby and a babysitter had allowed her to fall. Perhaps the child seemed unhurt at the time; but as the little limbs stretched and broadened, the infirmity grew painful. Sitting upright hurt much; in fact, holding the body still for any length of time pained her a great deal. Her hip and her twisted back were out of joint. She cried, but there was no loving mother to soothe and comfort her. Nellie's father at length realized that he could not carry on any longer in a motherless family, so he asked a kind priest friend to find a home in some convent for his forlorn orphans.

The parochial clergy came to his assistance, and, through their kind offices, each of the little ones was provided with a home in the charitable institutions of the diocese. Thomas was sent to the School of the Brothers of Charity at Upton; David, the younger brother, to the convent school of the Sisters of Mercy, Passage West; and it was arranged that Mary and Nellie should be sent to live at St.

Finbarr's* Industrial School conducted by the Sisters of the Good Shepherd at Sunday's Well, in the city of Cork, Ireland. With what truly maternal care the little girls were surrounded there will appear in the course of these pages.

Nellie was happy at the Good Shepherd, and she called all the Sisters "Mothers." Upon her arrival Nellie was three years and nine months old; she would live the remaining eight months of her life with the Sisters.

---

* Finbarr—also spelled Finbar.

∽ *Chapter 2* ∽

To the Good Shepherd Sisters

O N THE 11th of May, 1907, the two little sisters were brought to the convent. The resident nurse, Miss Hall, was immediately called to report upon the health of the little newcomers. She found that both were suffering from whooping cough, and medical opinion was deemed advisable. The doctor came at once, examined the children, and ordered their removal to the hospital.

The ambulance was immediately summoned. While awaiting the arrival of the ambulance, the nurse offered Nellie some soothing cough lozenges. The baby smiled through her tears at this and, taking the lozenges, offered them back to the nurse, saying, "Won't you take tum, too?" Miss Hall accepted one. Nellie then turned and offered the sweets to her sister. It was only when the others had begun to nibble theirs that she tasted a lozenge herself. What instinct was it that prompted such gracious behavior in a mere infant?

For about two months, until July 20, the Organ children remained in quarantine. When they were pronounced free from all contagion, they were allowed to return to the House of the Good Shepherd Sisters, Sunday's Well.

The 22nd of July was the feast of St. Mary Magdalen, a patron saint of the convent. During the Mass, Nellie insisted on facing the organ loft instead of the altar. The music thrilled her; her cheeks flushed as she stared toward the gallery. One of the older girls whispered to her that she must face the other way, but she stamped her foot and declared: "Me want to see the moosic nun!"

After Mass the children went into the dining room for breakfast. The tiny tots were served warm bread and milk sweetened with sugar. This was a much-loved dish called "goody"; but while the others ate heartily, Nellie could scarcely be persuaded to swallow a spoonful. It was then that the Sisters saw how frail she was. As the days passed, they noticed that the child walked and trotted unsteadily, with her arms held out before her as though she feared to fall.

They knew nothing of the injured back, caused by being dropped as a baby. But they saw that the regulation shoes were too heavy, so they got a fine pair of slipper shoes. Next day, dressed in white with rose-pink socks and her new shoes, Nellie looked quite a picture. Nellie's appearance was very striking because her coloring was quite unusual. Her fair hair framed a face set not with blue eyes as one might expect, but with great, luminous, solemn dark eyes. "She looked a little love," said a companion on this particular morning; "she looks like a little angel," said another.

Nellie was not all angel, though. A few days later, the "goody" served for breakfast proved unpalatable because the milk had been burned in cooking. Nellie sampled a spoonful from her share and made a grimace of disgust. Instead, however, of breaking forth into lamentations, as most children of her years would have done, she instantly slid from her perch, her little mug and spoon grasped firmly in both hands. Down the long dining hall she pitter-pattered between the rows of her staring companions, nor did she stop till she stood in the dignified presence of the nun who presided at the head of the room. Digging her small spoon into the disappointing mixture, she drew out a morsel and, holding it up in the face of the astonished Sister, demanded sturdily: "Mudder, tas'e dat!"

Another day, when the bell rang on the playground, the children went in for supper, but Nellie remained outside. Some of the children hid behind the trees to see what she would do. She went on quietly walking on a ladder that was on the ground. The next day the Sister told Nellie that she must not be naughty and keep the other children late for supper. "Dem could go if dey wanted," answered Nellie; "dem did go and leab me all alone."

"Are you sorry?" asked the Sister.

"Yes, I am sorry," answered Nellie.

"Then tell God you are." Instantly Nellie went on her knees.

"Holy Dod, I am berry, berry sorry for teeping de girls late for supper; please forgib me and make me a good child and bless me and my Mudders."

Obviously, Nellie already knew how to pray in her own words. Also, by the time she had arrived under the care of the Good Shepherd Sisters, Nellie could manage perfectly, in her own baby lisp, the Our Father, Hail Mary, Creed and Glory be.

∽ *Chapter 3* ∽

A Crooked Spine

FROM the beginning, Sister M. Immaculata, who was in charge of the children's wardrobe, was deeply interested in Little Nellie. She had set herself to study that little mind and heart and resolved to watch attentively every development in the character of her protegee. Nellie, she concluded, was an exceptionally intelligent child, affectionate and generous, and yet occasionally inclined to be peevish and self-willed. The little one gave way to frequent excesses of weeping, especially when bidden to sit still. This the Sister interpreted as manifesting a desire to have her own way, which she considered it was her duty to correct.

Sitting still was often the cause of bitter tears to Nellie on account of her crooked spine. One day she was particularly fractious. She wailed, cried and stamped her foot when they tried to soothe her. At last Sister M. Immaculata said to her reprovingly, "Come, come, Nellie, if you are not a good little girl, I will take off those pretty shoes and give you back your old ones." But Nellie redoubled her wailings. The Sister sent a pupil to take off the dainty shoes.

Meanwhile, Nellie's behavior puzzled Sister Immaculata. The child made no resistance to the girl's efforts; on the contrary, she assisted in removing the much-loved shoes and stockings and even managed a friendly smile, though the tears still trembled in the big mournful eyes. Presently, Nellie stole up to the Sister's knee and, clutching the folds of her habit, whispered softly, "Mudder, I am berry sorry." This was too much for Sister Immaculata. She caught up the little one in her arms and restored the socks and shoes. Nellie was a puzzle: these heroic efforts in such a baby to suppress tears and wailings which threatened to break out in spite of herself.

Then Mary Long, who slept next to Nellie, said that Nellie cried half the night and seemed to be suffering. Mary Long used to rise "every two hours" to warm little drinks of milk for Nellie, but nothing seemed to soothe her.

At last the Sister began to suspect that some physical deformity might account for Nellie's tantrums, so she examined the little frame minutely. Ah, there it was: a curved backbone, a crooked spine, throwing the limbs out of balance and involving much pain in certain postures.

The Sister was full of tender sympathy for the

little sufferer. Not long after, she was to have Nellie transferred to the restfulness of a comfortable bed in the school infirmary. There Nellie would share her meals with a little black kitten, of which she grew very fond and which fully reciprocated the child's affection. But alas, Nellie loved it so much that she nearly hugged the life out of it.

⮞ Chapter 4 ⮜

The Doctor's Diagnosis

CLASS lessons had now ceased for the crippled child, but she was taken at times to join the kindergarten games on the playground. One day she was given a box of beads to string. She put some in her mouth, and, something startling her, she swallowed, or rather half-swallowed them. They stuck in her throat and she seemed to be suffocating. The teacher snatched her up and went running to find the nurse.

Nurse and Sister arrived together. They rushed Nellie into the cottage hospital, also called the Sacred Heart Infirmary, on the convent grounds, and immediately performed the operation of extracting the beads. Five were removed from the neighborhood of the trachea. Nellie did not cry during the painful experience, but sometime later she seemed to collapse. They sent for the doctor. With grief in their hearts they heard his diagnosis: Nellie was already the victim of the dread disease that had proved fatal to her mother. The doctor held out no hope whatever of her recovery.

In fact, he assured the Sister that the child had not many months to live.

Sister Immaculata's heart was pierced with regret for what she called her "harshness" to the suffering child. Nellie seemed to be instinctively aware of what was passing in the Sister's mind. One evening, soon after the doctor's visit, she expressed a wish to see "Mudder 'Lata" and also the Mother Superior. Both hastened immediately to the cottage. We are told by Fr. Scannell that "two very busy nuns" both obeyed her summons and arrived together. But Nellie, after a gracious smile to the Superior, turned and threw her arms around Sister Immaculata's neck, drawing her down and holding her close, her little cheek laid caressingly against that of the nun. For quite a considerable time she held her mistress in that close embrace but spoke no word whatever. The Mother Superior was puzzled, but Sister knew in her heart that the little scene was intended by Nellie as an assurance of her full forgiveness and forgetfulness of the past.

∽ Chapter 5 ∽

Nellie and the Infant Jesus

THE little invalid remained for two months in the Sacred Heart Infirmary. Nurse frequently considered it advisable to pass the night with her, and Nellie's gratitude for this attention was full of childlike pathos. "Holy Dod took my Mudder," she would say, "but He has gib'n me you to be my Mudder." She would put out her tiny hand between the rails of her crib to take that of her "Mudder," and she would clasp it affectionately until the little fingers gradually relaxed and she fell into a fitful sleep.

While Nellie was still confined to bed in the Sacred Heart Infirmary, a little altar on which stood a statue of the Holy Infant of Prague attracted her attention. Nurse (Miss Hall) explained to her that the statue was an image of Our Lord when He was a child. Immediately Nellie's interest was aroused. Nurse proceeded to narrate the story of the birth of Christ and His great love for us. The child listened with evident enthusiasm, and ever afterward she delighted in

15

"the story of Holy God when He was a little child."

From that moment she turned with all the sweet simplicity of childhood and spoke to little Jesus. Soon she made a novena to Him, at the suggestion of the nuns, asking Him to make her well. When the novena was ended, she unexpectedly became so far recovered as to be able to walk about in the garden holding someone's hand. Naturally, this inspired in her a great confidence in the Holy Child, with whom she now began to chat familiarly and of whom she made the most extraordinary demands.

When, shortly afterwards, Nurse Hall became unwell, Nellie called one of the senior girls and said to her, "Go an' bring me Holy God, an' put Him on de chair near me. I want to ask Him to make Mudder better. He made me better, you know."

Among Nellie's toys was a tin whistle. Many were the tunes and trills that she, with her perfect sense of rhythm, could produce therefrom. One day toward the end of September, Mary Long was busy in the kitchen of the cottage infirmary, where Nellie still resided. Mary was engaged in copying some verses which the children were to recite on the occasion of a visit from the Mother Provincial, who was expected daily. Nellie was there, too, playing quietly with her toys. Presently she came over to Mary and coaxed: "Longie, div me my baby," for that is how she always spoke of the little statue of the Infant of Prague. Mary paid no heed at first, but Nellie went on: "Longie, div me my baby," until Mary, to have peace, said: "I will give it to you, Nellie, but please do not break it or Mother Francis will be vexed."

Mary went into the other room, got the statue, and gave it to Nellie. Nellie, now perfectly happy and content, hugged the little image, hushing it in her arms and kissing it, with many lisping murmurs of affectionate address. Then she put it on the floor beside the pots and pans. Mary went on with her copying. Let us now continue in Mary Long's own words:

"Presently Nellie gets very excited and calls out: 'Longie, Him dance for me! Longie, play moosic,' and she snatches hold of her whistle and keeps on blowing, only stopping to cry, 'Him dance for me! Longie, play more moosic!' I thought the child had gone mad. Then Josephine, the girl who helped with the cleaning, came in. Josephine at once said, 'What is the matter with Nellie?' Nellie, her face flushed, her eyes sparkling, cries out—just flinging one glance toward us, then instantly back again to the statue—'Jo! play moosic: Him dance for me; now me dance for Him,' and Nellie begins stepping about, her arms extended. Stopping suddenly, she cries in a disappointed little voice, 'Oh, Him 'topped now!' And she is quiet once more."

That evening Nurse Hall found Nellie all flushed and running a fever. Nellie had grown so weak and ill that it was feared she would die, so she was carried to the school infirmary, which was brighter and more cheerful than the cottage. That evening, while the nurse was carrying her off, Nellie kept repeating, "Him dance for me, and me dance for Him! Him dance for me, and me dance for Him!" until the nurse sent angrily to Mary Long, asking who had been to the cottage to excite Nellie so much. Mary answered, "No one has been to the cottage." Reverend Mother then came over to the school infirmary. To her Nellie kept up the same refrain: "Him dance for me, and me dance for Him!" Reverend Mother in her turn sent word indignantly to Mary: "Tell Mary Long I want to know what man has been to the cottage." Poor Mary sent the same reply as before: "No man. No one at all." But she added some account of the alleged dance and the strange behavior of Little Nellie.

Nellie's rapturous refrain and the shining, trembling happiness that shook her were beginning to impress the spiritually attuned nun. She, too, had a great devotion to the Holy Child, and soon afterward, passing by a statue of the Infant of Prague, she dropped on her knees with a simple prayer: "Lord, if You really did dance for Little Nellie, please send us a bakehouse."

A bakehouse was something that the Sisters badly needed. A bakehouse would enable them to make bread for themselves and all those in their care instead of undergoing the continuing expense of purchasing large quantities of bread. But alas, the Sisters were already in debt for additions to their original premises, so a bakehouse was out of the question.

A few days later the community was amazed when a lady sent them a check for three hundred pounds* marked: "For a bakehouse."

One more incident testifies to Nellie's great trust in the Child Jesus: One day in the cloister Nellie stopped before a statue of Our Lady and the Divine Child with the world in His hand. "If You gib' me Your ball," said Nellie, "I'll gib' You my little shoeses." Nurse said: "Nellie, you can't get that." "Him can gib' 'em if Him likes," answered Nellie confidently.

---

* In today's money, 300 Irish pounds would be equivalent to many thousands of dollars.

Actual photo of Nellie near the end of her life. Although its
quality is poor, the photo shows Nellie's intelligence and
intensity. Those who knew Nellie said that she seemed to
see right through a person.

This appears to be a retouched photo or a painting of Nellie on her First Communion day. This picture came from the Good Shepherd Convent in St. Paul, Minnesota.

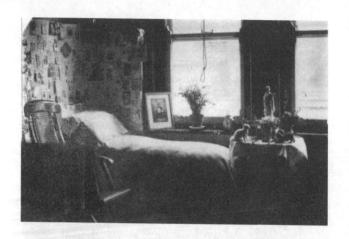

Above: Nellie's room shortly after she died.
Below: The Old Infirmary, where Nellie spent some time. She died in Nurse Hall's apartment, where she had spent the last four months of her life.

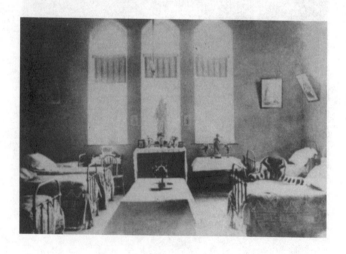

The altar and altar rail in the Good Shepherd Convent
Chapel, Sunday's Well, before which Nellie made her First
Holy Communion on December 6, 1907.

Above and Below: Nellie's sister, Mary.

Above: One of Nellie's brothers.
Left and Below: A nephew and two nieces of Nellie.

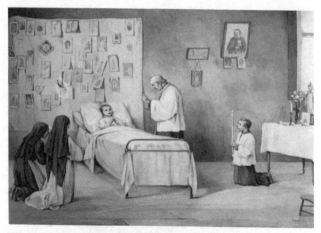

When Nellie was too ill to go down to the chapel, Holy Communion was brought to her in her room, where an altar of the sick would be prepared.

A year and a week after Nellie's death, the grave was opened. Her body was found to be exactly as it was on the day of her death. *(Images on this page courtesy of Gus Nugent and Leo Madigan).*

John Donovan, Dungarvan, Co. Waterford

Above: The Convent of the Good Shepherd in Sunday's Well, Cork, Ireland, after the fire. The Convent burned down in 2003, having stood empty for a few years previous. *Below:* An early tribute to Nellie engraved on marble.

Leo Madigan

Nellie's grave in the cemetery of the Good Shepherd Convent, Sunday's Well, Cork City. The cemetery is intact and can still be visited, although the old convent is no longer standing.

The inscription on Nellie's monument reads: "In loving memory of Little Nellie of Holy God, who died February 2nd, 1908. R.I.P. Suffer the little children to come unto Me. Mark 10:14. Pray for the donor." The French plaque bears this message: In remembrance of Little Nellie, France, 1932.

Leo Madigan

Pope St. Pius X, who reigned as Pope from 1903-1914. Nellie prayed for Pius X and called him "my own Holy Father." Pope Pius X took office on August 4, 1903. Nellie was born on August 24, 1903.

∽ *Chapter 6* ∽

"Holy God"

WHEN Nellie's health permitted, Nurse occasionally carried her to the garden. On the way there the two usually paid a visit to the convent chapel. Nellie looked forward to these visits; she knew that this was "the House of Holy God, where the people went who wanted to speak to Him."

Sometimes Nurse would make the Way of the Cross holding Nellie in her arms. Nellie would fix her earnest, inquiring gaze on the different pictures of the Sacred Passion. Once, when Nurse came to the picture of the Crucifixion, Nellie became very agitated.

"Why am dey doin' dat?" she asked, shuddering.

Nurse explained briefly that "Holy God wished to suffer for our sins."

"But why did Him allow 'em hurt Him?" responded the child. "Him could stop 'em."

Nurse took the child aside and explained to her as simply as possible the goodness of Christ and all He suffered in His Sacred Passion. Nellie lis-

30

tened with deep attention, and when Nurse had
finished the story of Calvary, she burst into tears,
exclaiming between her sobs: "Poor Holy God!
Poor Holy God!" This expression would become
Nellie's watchword in suffering.

Meanwhile, her suffering from thirst became
extreme. At night she would call the attendant
and ask in her sad, pleading voice for "a little sup
o' milk." If the girl did not hear her first entreaty,
Nellie would not call again, fearing to disturb her
rest, but would wait patiently until morning. At
last, however, the suffering became intolerable,
and the little one begged of the Nurse to stay near
her at night. Nurse readily consented, and had
her bed prepared beside Nellie's in the infirmary.
The child superintended these arrangements and
insisted on smoothing the sheets with her own little hands: "I don't want any wrinkles in Mudder's
bed," she said.

This new arrangement gave Nellie ample
opportunities for those little spiritual conversa-
tions which she loved so much. Nurse, a recent
convert to the Catholic Faith, often found it difficult to frame an answer to Nellie's questions; she
confessed that she frequently had to ask for information from the Sisters. But also, more than once
the little one's remarks so impressed her that she
then accepted without further demur certain
points of Catholic doctrine and practice concern-

ing which she had found it difficult to overcome her former prejudices.

Nellie had already grasped the truth that God was present in the Tabernacle. The Mystery of the Real Presence seemed to have made a deep impression on her young mind. Once, during a visit to the chapel, she questioned Nurse about it. "Why am Holy God shut up in dat little house?" she asked. Nurse found some difficulty in explaining that He was present there under the sacramental species. The child, however, seemed to understand. She was glad that "Holy God was not 'squeezeded' in dat little house."

Nellie seemed to live in the presence of God in the highest and truest sense, so intimately did she speak of "Holy God," and this wonderful intimacy increased accordingly as her bodily health declined.

They brought flowers to Nellie to while away the dreary days of illness. True to her mother's training, no doubt, she instantly associated them with their first cause. "Isn't Holy God good," she would cry, "to have made such lobly flowers for me?" She hated artificial flowers. "Dey are too 'tiff (stiff)," she used to say; "bring me some of Holy God's own flowers."

One day Mary Long, on reaching the door of the infirmary, was surprised to find Nellie scrambling back into bed, in her hand a flower which she had evidently taken from a vase that stood on a table nearby. Perceiving Mary, Nellie slipped the flower under the bed clothes, believing her action to be unobserved. But Mary had seen it and began questioning the child: "Who stole that lovely daisy from the vase?"

"No one, Longie."

"Then where is it? Perhaps it is under the bed?"—and Mary pretended to be searching about for it. With a shriek of laughter, Nellie produced it from its hiding place. What a good joke that was, to be sure.

"Oh, you naughty child," said the girl. I'll tell Mother, when she comes back, that you stole a flower." Nellie did not answer for a moment but hugged the flower to her breast, then quietly remarked that the altar was hers. Later, when she was alone with Nurse, Nellie said to her, "Mudder, I'm sorry I took de flower; but I was only talking to Holy God, and Him dived me de flower, Him did, Mudder."

Once Nellie noticed some dead flowers by the Sacred Heart statue outside the infirmary. She spoke up: "Look at dem dirty flowers, dem must be taken away." Long afterward, when she was so weak that she could not leave her bed, she frequently asked Reverend Mother whether "dem dirty flowers" had been taken away from the statue of Holy God.

~ Chapter 7 ~

Holy God in the
Blessed Sacrament

MARY Long,* not sleeping well at night, did not always feel able to rise for the community Mass next morning. On one such occasion, when Nellie was still living in the cottage, she remained quietly in the kitchen until she heard the children pass into their refectory after Mass. Then she opened the door to Nellie's room and said, "Well, Nellie, how are you today?"

To her surprise, Nellie answered reproachfully, "You did not get Holy God dis morning."

Mary thought that perhaps Nellie had heard her moving about in the kitchen. Accordingly, an idea occurred to her to test Nellie next time. She went to the door of the cottage, opened the latch, and closed the door again, thus giving the impression, as she thought, that she had really gone to Mass. She then removed her boots, and during

_____

* Another source recounts this same story but gives "Katie" as the name of the girl involved.

34

Mass time she moved about as little as possible in the kitchen. When she returned to Nellie's room, she looked quite unconcerned. The child, however, fixed her pensive eyes on Mary's countenance, and then the same reproving words were spoken sadly:

"You did not get Holy God today."

"How do you know, lovey?" said Mary. "Didn't you hear me close the door?"

"No matter," said the child, "I know you didn't get Holy God."

Nurse Hall gave the following account of Nellie's extraordinary behavior on the occasion of her first visit to the chapel during Exposition of the Blessed Sacrament.

Nurse carried Nellie down to the chapel. Nellie had never before actually seen the Sacred Host exposed in the monstrance. What then was Miss Hall's surprise to hear the little one say to her in an awed whisper: "Mudder, there He is, there is Holy God now! And with her little hand she pointed to the monstrance, after which she never once took her eyes off the Host, while an expression of ecstasy transfigured her face.

In another account of this same first visit, Reverend Mother writes: "It was the First Friday of the month (October), I was passing along the corridor, when the chapel door opened and Nellie, holding the Nurse's hand, toddled out softly and recollectedly. Remembering how ill the child had been, I stooped down, one knee on the floor, and said: 'Well, how is Baby today?' For answer the little one laid her face on my shoulder and wept silently; but her tears were not sad, they were all sweetness; it was a holy emotion, the happiness of which overflowed in wordless weeping. In that moment," continues the Mother solemnly, "it was made known to me interiorly that God had some special designs on the child, and that I, then Superior, was expected to co-operate with Him in accomplishing them."

From that day onward, by some interior warning, without a single exterior sign to guide her, Nellie always knew when there was Exposition at the convent.

Nellie had been born in the army barracks, where the prison was called the "lock-up." So she regarded Jesus as a "Prisoner" in the "lock-up." On Exposition days she would say: "Take me down to the chapel. I know that Holy God is not in the lock-up today."

❧ *Chapter 8* ❧

Confirmation

FILLED with a sense of her responsibility before God, the Reverend Mother pondered how she could conform to the Will of God in the matter of Little Nellie's spiritual advancement. She knew that the child had not long to live; the doctor had already said so, and clearly she was worse now than when the doctor had pronounced judgment a month previously. The Mother recalled, too, how the Most Reverend Dr. O'Callaghan, O.P., Bishop of Cork, had told her that if any of the children were in danger of death, she was to inform him, and he would come and administer the Sacrament of Confirmation. "The graces of the Sacrament," he used to say, "will make a great difference to God's glory and the soul's degree of bliss in Heaven." Being fearful of troubling him, however, with an unusual request—for this child was a mere baby, and perhaps His Lordship had in mind children of a more advanced age—the good nun forbore mentioning Little Nellie to the Bishop.

Still, she was not happy. She felt self-reproach-ful. She betook herself to prayer. Then, as it hap-pened, the Bishop wrote to her, making some inquiry into the affairs of an aged person in whom he was interested. In writing her reply, the Rev-erend Mother mentioned the two Organs by name as the two latest lambs to be admitted to the Good Shepherd's flock. She added that Nellie, just arrived at the age of four, was very fragile; but Reverend Mother made no suggestion at all of Confirmation.

On reading the nun's letter, the Bishop took no particular notice of the paragraph concerning Lit-tle Nellie, but the next morning—so he himself affirms—he "felt inspired during Holy Mass to go and confirm Nellie Organ."

Immediately after breakfast he rang up the Superior and told her he proposed coming at twelve o'clock that very day to administer the Sacrament of Confirmation to Nellie Organ.

That news, of course, set the whole convent in a flutter. While Sister Immaculata was engrossed in the selection of material things like the white frock, wreath, veil, gloves and dainty wear, another Sister hurried upstairs bent on giving Nellie some religious instruction on the nature of the Sacrament she was about to receive. To the Sister's amazement, she found that Nellie already knew all that she had intended teaching her. The same Sister tells us that, as the moment for her Confirmation approached, Nellie's limbs trembled from the excess of her joyful anticipation.

And so, on October 8, 1907, Nellie received the Seven Gifts of the Holy Spirit. Afterward she was brought to the parlor to be introduced to the good Bishop. It was then that the Bishop, as he afterward declared, was so impressed by the graces which he now perceived had been granted to this orphan child. Nellie declared to all who came to see her on her Confirmation day: "I am now a soldier of Holy God."

The afternoon of the Confirmation day was very pleasant for the little one. Miss Hall had made for her a soft down bed in her own apartment. There Nellie held quite a reception: all the community of Sisters, all the children came in groups to visit her, and sweets and "goodies" were passed around. When late evening fell, the Sister in charge sent a grown girl to carry Nellie back to the school infirmary, but Nellie pleaded so hard to be left with her second mother that the kind Superior could not refuse. So it was in Miss Hall's room that the child spent all the rest of her mortal days. In this room she gave back her snow-white soul to her Creator. This little room was for a long time preserved in the Convent of Sunday's Well exactly as on the day she left it. All her toys were left there—the bunny rabbit and the tin bugle; all her little pictures and objects of piety; the statue of the Divine Infant of Prague—everything that she had loved and handled.

Mother Francis was witness to the spiritual effects of the Sacrament of Confirmation in Nellie. Years later she recalled:

"I was privileged to watch the petals of virtue unfold under the warm sunshine of God's grace in this precious soul. Nellie had a temper, to be sure, and when provoked she would stomp her little feet and the large dark eyes would flash fire. But after she received the Sacrament of Confirmation with its sevenfold gifts, I never saw her give way to her temper. The eyes would flash and the tears would fall, but, valiant little soldier of Christ that she now was, she never lost the battle."

∽ *Chapter 9* ∽

Nellie's "Sore Throat"

SOON after her Confirmation, the child's appetite, always small, seemed to fail completely. She would hold her little bowl of broth or milk, turning and turning the spoon about in it, but refusing to eat. When pressed to swallow some, she tried to comply, but swallowing evidently hurt her; and she would shake her head and say her "t'roat" was sore.

The doctor was called to examine Nellie's throat but could find nothing wrong. Nellie heard his opinion calmly, did not cry over it, nor over her pain, but continued to assert nevertheless that her "t'roat" was sore. Finally the little mouth was explored thoroughly, and a new tooth was discovered that had just cut its way through at the root of the tongue—entirely in the wrong place, of course, but there it was. The truth is that poor Nellie had a diseased jaw; and the tooth, cutting through at such a point, must have caused her very serious pain. Yet she did not cry while it was being removed.

41

In all this tale of the tooth it is Nellie's bearing that interests us. She had borne in silence to be called "pettish" and so on, when the doctor failed to discover anything wrong. The doctor, however, was examining her *throat,* not realizing that his little patient was too young to name specifically the area of her suffering.

Now, however, that she had been proved in the right, she drove it home to the Mother Superior with charming sweetness. She looked forward quite excitedly to Reverend Mother's evening visit; then, holding her by the sleeve and, smilingly triumphant, Nellie said: "Now, Mudder, hadn't I a sore throat, hadn't I?" until Mother Superior kissed her and agreed.

Mother Francis Xavier had instructed Nellie concerning the significance of the crucifix. Here is Mary Long's reminiscence: "The prioress, Mother Francis Xavier Hickey, used to come over to see Nellie every evening. Then Mother would kneel by Nellie, take out her crucifix, and explain Our Lord's life. . . ."

All this time, tuberculosis was wasting away the baby frame. Not only were Nellie's lungs affected, but her jawbone had begun to crumble away from the disease known as "caries." In the end it came away in pieces, and the odor from it was extremely unpleasant—at times unbearable. The devoted nurse syringed it frequently with disinfectants. This, although it hurt considerably, was nevertheless not once resisted by the child after her Confirmation. When the nurse took out her syringe, Nellie took out her crucifix. Giving her intelligent consent to this pain, which clearly God had laid upon her, she thought of the Great Atonement. When the pain was greatest she used to lie motionless in bed, her arms crossed on her breast, her little fingers folded around her crucifix.

The comparative maturity of Nellie's mind is borne out by the manner in which her little companions regarded her. "The children were a little afraid of Nellie," we are told. "She seemed to know so much for such a baby." All agreed that Nellie was truthful, that she never told tales, and that she was extraordinarily serious for her years.

∽ Chapter 10 ∽

An Extraordinary
Conversation

ONE morning, Sister Immaculata and
Nurse Hall went together to visit the
little patient, who had spent a very rest-
less night. It was then that the following extraordinary conversation took place:

"How are you today, darling?" asked the nurse.
"I thought that you would have been with Holy
God by this time."

"Oh, no!" answered Nellie, "Holy God says I am
not good enough to go yet."

"What do you know about Holy God?" asked
Nurse.

"Him did come an' stand dere," replied the
child, pointing to the side of her bed, "and Him did
say dat."

Nurse and the Sister looked at each other in
amazement.

"Where was He, Nellie?" asked the Sister.

"Dere," she repeated confidently, pointing to the
same spot.

"And what was He like?" asked the Sister again.

"Like dat," answered Nellie, putting her hands on her breast in a tucked position.

Sister and Nurse were naturally astounded at this revelation. Was it a childish fancy or had God favored this little child as He had favored other chosen souls? After much deliberation, they agreed that it would be more prudent not to mention the matter to anyone, unless Nellie herself should speak of it again. We shall see that little Nellie, when on the threshold of eternity, solemnly repeated the story of this visit of Holy God.

～ Chapter 11 ～

Growth in Grace

FOR so young a child, little Nellie had made marvelous progress in religious knowledge. She had learned by heart the morning and evening prayers, the acts of faith, hope and charity, the principal mysteries of religion, and much of the story of the life of Jesus.

Her growth in holiness was even more remarkable. She manifested a wonderful devotion to the Passion of Our Divine Lord, and when they exhorted her to unite her sufferings with those of the Redeemer, she seemed to grasp the idea immediately and was quite prepared to make the heroic sacrifice and to endure the most atrocious suffering without a murmur of complaint. She kept a crucifix beside her on her bed, and when her sufferings became almost unbearable, she would take it in her little hand, stare at it fixedly, and whisper, "Poor Holy God! Oh, poor Holy God!" If others sympathized with her, she would smile and remark, "What is it compared with what He suffered on the Cross for me?"

Sometimes Nellie's kind visitors brought her little delicacies, which she accepted gratefully. She partook of a little in order to show that she appreciated their attention. But when her friends were gone, the good things they had brought were laid aside, to be afterward shared with others.

She prayed fervently during the day, and her earnestness and recollection were most edifying. She prayed for all who were dear to her—the Sisters, the Bishop, Nurse, her little companions; and daily that pleading voice was raised to Heaven for the welfare of the Church of Christ and His Vicar on earth.

Nellie's recital of the Rosary was particularly edifying. She kissed each of the large beads and the crucifix and recited each prayer slowly, distinctly, and with a spirit of recollection most remarkable in one so young.

"One evening," writes Reverend Mother, "while I was sitting beside her bed, I said to her: 'Shall I talk to you, Baby, or shall we say the Rosary?'

"'Say the Rosary, Mudder,' she answered. I had only said a few Hail Marys when I heard her whisper, 'Kneel down, Mudder.' I paid no attention and continued to the end of the first decade, when she repeated in quite a determined tone, 'Kneel down, Mudder,' and I had to finish the Rosary on my knees."

Another day while saying the Rosary, when the

fifth Mystery was reached, the child interrupted: "Mudder, let us say dis one for de Pope, for *my* Holy Fadder," and this was done. Then the litany followed, and when the Sign of the Cross had been made, Nellie took her crucifix and kissed it solemnly. "Dis kiss is for *my* Pope, for *my own* Holy Fadder,"* she explained.

---

* Another source gives *Pader* as Nellie's pronunciation of "Father."

∽ *Chapter 12* ∽

Longing to Receive Holy God

THE Sisters, who first were amazed to behold Nellie's desire to be carried down to the presence of the Blessed Sacrament, were now still more surprised to hear her sighs of longing for the then unheard-of privilege in childhood of receiving Holy Communion. Often now she was heard repeating to herself: "Oh, I am longing for Holy God! I wonder when He will come! I am longing to have Him in my heart."

Reverend Mother visited Nellie every evening. On one occasion, when about to bid the child "Good night," she was startled by the following request. "Mudder," asked Nellie, "tomorrow morning, when you get Holy God, will you bring Him up to me?" Mother knew not what to answer. She considered for a moment and then replied, "Tomorrow morning I shall ask Holy God to be very fond of you, and I shall come up to see you after Mass." This reply seemed to satisfy the child. Later in the evening she called Nurse Hall and said to her, "Mudder Prancis is goin' to bring me Holy God in de mornin'."

Before daybreak Nellie was awake. She woke the nurse by calling incessantly: "Mudder! Mudder! Please get up an' clean de house 'cause Holy God is comin' up to me today." Nurse tried to calm her, saying, "Josephine will be over soon, darling." But Nellie was not satisfied. "Jo am late dis mornin'," she replied; "de place will never be ready." Nurse had to get up. Nellie followed her with watchful eyes while she tidied the room. If she stopped a moment, the little voice began again: "Mudder, what am you doin'? De place will never be ready!"

As Mass hour drew near, Nellie watched for the coming of Reverend Mother with eagerness. When she saw Mother Francis enter without "Holy God," her disappointment was so keen that she wept bitterly.

During the rest of that day Nellie scarcely spoke a word. In the evening she said to Nurse with a heavy sigh, "Mudder, I did t'ink I would hab' had Holy God today."

For some days after that sorrowful experience, Nellie lay sad, not caring to talk or play. Sometimes she would sigh wistfully, and when they asked if she needed anything, she would answer: "No, I am just t'inking about Holy God."

Soon, however, the clever little brain had evolved a plan which might solace—though it could not satisfy—her longing for Holy Communion.

"Mudder," she whispered to the nurse one morning, "when you get Holy God in de chapel, will you come back an' kiss me? Den you can go back to the chapel again."

This kiss was not for Nurse, it was for the Blessed Sacrament. It was given indiscriminately to anyone, nun or child or grown-up, whom Nellie could coax to come to her immediately after their receiving Holy Communion. In profound reverence the baby lips would touch the lips of the communicant, then in strictest silence she would wave her tiny hand as a signal to the other to return and finish her thanksgiving. Sometimes Nurse would hesitate to leave Nellie to attend Mass, but Nellie would always insist. "Mudder, go down to Mass," she would say, "an' get Holy God an' come back to kiss me. Den you can go back to de chapel again."

The whole month of November passed thus in holy desire, in suffering patiently borne, and in loving thoughts of Jesus in the Blessed Sacrament.

∼ *Chapter 13* ∼

First Communion

THE Sisters had begun a ten-day retreat which was to end on December 8, the Feast of the Immaculate Conception. Fr. Bury, S.J., was the director. Naturally, the Sisters mentioned to him the longing for Holy Communion of the "extraordinary child" upstairs. This, of course, was before Pope St. Pius X's decree concerning the First Communion of little children. At this time children generally were not admitted to Holy Communion until ten or twelve years of age.

Father Bury, far from dismissing the Sisters' account, gave his sympathetic attention. "St. Alphonsus," he said, "gave Holy Communion to a tiny child who longed for it. If the Bishop permitted me, I would do the same by Little Nellie."

Fr. Bury went up and had a talk with Nellie. "What is the Blessed Eucharist?" he asked. Nellie's reply was all her own: there was not a touch of coaching or catechism about it. "It is Holy God," she lisped; "it is Him dat makes de nuns and everybody else holy." On another occasion she would say, "Jesus comes on my tongue and goes down into my heart." The words were indeed the words of an infant, but the doctrine was profound.

Father Bury wrote a letter to the Bishop requesting permission to give this little child the Bread of Angels. According to Father Bury, "With regard to the reception of this Sacrament, Nellie had arrived at the use of reason." He told the Bishop that Nellie was endowed in no ordinary degree with ardent love of God and the desire to be united to Him in Holy Communion.

The answer came while Father Bury was dining in the convent parlor. No sooner had he read the permission than he started up from his unfinished meal, flung his napkin halfway across the table and rushed upstairs two steps at a time to take the joyful news to the anxious little one.

When Nellie heard the glad tidings, her joy was indescribable. "I will hab' Holy God in my heart, I will hab' Holy God in my heart"—such was the burden of all she said that day.

And now she goes to Confession! We may well ask what such a mite had to confess. The thought makes us, who are sinners, smile tolerantly. Yet Father Bury made it clear to the nuns that Nellie had validly received the Sacrament of Penance— a certain sign, this, that he judged her dispositions proper and her contrition supernatural. "She was interiorly illumined by God," Bishop O'Callaghan had said; therefore, she saw sin as the Saints see it, and like another Aloysius she wept with sorrow for some childish aberration. Often after that first Confession Nellie could be heard begging God to pardon her her "sins."

The night before her First Communion day brought Nellie little rest; she could not sleep for joy. She kept Nurse awake all night long, asking if it were not yet time to rise. "De stars are gone, Mudder!" she would cry, "'tis time to get up now."

The eventful morning dawned at last, the morning of December 6, 1907. After such a sleepless night it was feared the excitement would be too much for the delicate child and that she would be unable to receive the Blessed Sacrament. But Nellie tried to calm herself; she lay quietly in her bed, and though her limbs trembled slightly, the illness passed.

It was the First Friday. Dressed all in white, she was carried down and placed in a little easy chair before the Sanctuary. The community Mass had just ended. Nellie remained silent and motionless with her head bowed down in prayer and adoration. Every eye was on this baby of predilection; all her companions looked on in wonder. A baby to receive Holy Communion!

Then came Father Bury in stole and surplice.

"Domine non sum dignus"—"Lord, I am not worthy." Who can be worthy? No one. But He can make us worthy by His gifts and graces. Nellie knew this well, for He Himself had taught her. She saw the priest approaching, she lifted her eager face. "The child," wrote Father Bury, "literally hungered for her God, and received Him from my hands in a transport of love."

So all of Nellie's yearnings were satisfied. Holy God had come into her heart at last.

The joyous strains of the First Communion Hymn echoed:

> O Mary, dearest Mother,
> In God's sweet scented bowers,
> Will you gather for a little child
> A wreath of fragrant flowers.
>   Chorus:
> I wish my heart to be
> A cradle fair and gay,
> Where my Blessed Jesus may repose
> On my First Communion Day.

The hymn is now dedicated to Pope St. Pius X and called "Nellie's First Communion Hymn."

A priest wrote in October, 1911, describing Nellie's thanksgiving after her First Communion. "The happy moment will long be remembered by those who had the privilege of being present. Nellie seemed in an ecstasy, and all remarked the heavenly light that lighted up the child's countenance."

And Fr. Scannell recounted, "Still she sat there motionless, insensible to things of earth, in silent, loving conference with the Saviour, her radiant countenance reflecting the Eternal Light within her."

After her First Communion, Nellie was brought back to her bed in Nurse's room. All day long the child maintained that profound calm which is rarely met with except in souls of more than ordinary sanctity. Many of the Sisters and her companions visited her; they brought her gifts of pictures, scapulars and medals. She thanked them quietly and bade Nurse hang them around her bed. The moment the visitors had gone, she joined her hands in prayer, and her lips were seen to move, whispering her love and gratitude to Holy God.

And then a strange thing was noticed: the disagreeable (some said, you may remember, "the unbearable") odor that previously had exhaled from the diseased jaw was never experienced again after that First Communion morning.

On the following Sunday, Nellie again received Holy Communion, and the same scene of holy pathos moved the hearts of those who witnessed it. After Benediction, Nellie was enrolled in the

Sodality of the Children of Mary. Her deportment during the ceremony was extraordinarily dignified and calm. Her brilliant eyes followed the chaplain's every movement, while her lips moved continually in silent prayer. At the given signal she raised her little head and received the ribbon and medal, the holy livery of Mary, with great devotion.

The next day, December 9, Nellie was anointed. Death seemed to be at hand momentarily, and the grace of Extreme Unction was now added to the graces she had already received. The Sisters said to one another: "Our little Nellie has received all the Sacraments except Holy Orders and Matrimony."

Yet Nellie did not die. She continued to live on, so weak as oftentimes to be unfit for the slight fatigue of being carried down to the chapel for Holy Communion. Yet unless it were physically impossible, she insisted on being carried to "the House of Holy God."

Only when her sufferings were most intense would the little martyr whisper sadly, "Mudder, I'm too tired to go down to Holy God today." Then Holy Communion was brought to her in her room, where an altar for the sick could readily be prepared. When she received in the convent chapel, her thanksgiving edified even those consecrated souls who had spent long years in the loving ser-

vice of their Heavenly Spouse. When the Blessed
Sacrament was brought to her as she lay in her
bed, she received with still greater fervor.

Chapter 14

Nellie's Preparation and Thanksiving for Holy Communion

NELLIE would receive Holy God about 32 times in all. On the evening before, she would become absorbed in meditation; and when she awoke the next morning, her thoughts, it would appear, were all of Holy God. She would not speak an unnecessary word before she had welcomed Jesus to her heart. She even asked her nurse not to speak to her until after Mass.

"I had heard so much about Nellie's preparation for and thanksgiving after Holy Communion," writes Sister Mary of St. Francis de Sales, "and much of what I had heard seemed to me so incredible in one so young, that I determined to judge the matter for myself. Accordingly, I went one morning to her room. When the priest entered, Nellie immediately fixed her eyes with a look of love on the pyx which he held in his hands and did not move them from it while he was preparing to administer Holy Communion.

"Scarcely had she received when her face underwent a complete transformation; a supernatural expression diffused itself on her countenance, her head fell back on the pillow, and she grew pale as death. I could detect no movement in that little body, and I thought for the moment that she had expired. The reason, however, was that she knew so well what the Blessed Sacrament is, and what He was whom she then received into her heart, that the intensity of love and gratitude overwhelmed her, and she became insensible to things of earth."

Nellie's longing for the Bread of Angels was insatiable. One night she, who as a rule was so patient, kept Nurse awake, continually calling out: "I want Holy God, I want Holy God. Mudder, will it soon be mornin'?"

"Try to sleep," answered Nurse. "Father won't be here for a long time yet."

"Go an' call him," begged Nellie, "an' tell him I want Holy God. Does he lib' in de garden, Mudder?"

Nurse answered: "He lives a long way off in the city." At last morning came, and Nellie's desire was satisfied.

This was the time when her thanksgiving lasted till evening. When Mother Superior visited her at a quarter to five, she was lying quite still, turned toward the window. Mother related:

"I had heard of her strange condition during

the day, and was very curious to see her. I bent over her, and as I did so, Nellie turned suddenly around and said, 'O Mudder, I'm so happy. I've been talking to Holy God.' Her voice trembled with delight; her face, previously so dusky with the ravages of disease, was now white as milk. Her cheeks glowed (I can best express what I mean by saying) 'as a smiling peach.' Her large eyes shone with such brilliancy that one could not help thinking, 'These eyes have seen God.' Her smile cannot be described because it was of Heaven, and around the bed was the distinct aroma of incense." (This extraordinary fact is also attested by another witness.)

Nellie's love of purity displayed itself especially in her preparation for receiving the Bread of Angels. She insisted that everything should be spotlessly white when Holy God was to come to visit her: her garments, the bedspread, even the flowers on her little altar of the sick. On one occasion she told Sister Mary of St. Ursula that she could not receive Holy Communion unless she was wearing her white frock. Sister Mary of St. Ursula, who had charge of Nellie's laundry, told her she should be satisfied this once with a colored flannel one, but Nellie insisted: "No, I want de white one; I can't get Holy God in dis dress." When Sister finally satisfied her wishes, Nellie joyfully exclaimed, "Now I am able to get Holy God!"

⌒ *Chapter 15* ⌒

Christmas

I N THE forenoon of Christmas Eve, Nellie was brought to the chapel to see the crib. She was delighted with the different figures and kissed the statue of the Divine Infant with reverence and love. Returning to her room, she insisted on having a Christmas crib of her own. They found her a statue of the Holy Child and arranged a little crib on the table beside her bed. Nellie superintended the arrangements and sent Nurse's assistant to get some straw "to make a bed for Holy God." The girl returned and announced that she could not find any. "Dere's plenty down in de farmyard," said Nellie, and the girl had to go back to renew her search. Finally the straw was found, and Nellie, aided by Nurse, prepared "the bed for Holy God." She herself opened out the straw, that there might be "no lumps in Holy God's bed." Then the statue of the Infant Saviour was laid in the crib, holding a little branch of holly in its hand.

Nellie had tried to rest early in the evening, but

long before the hour for Holy Communion had arrived, she was making her preparation. "Do not speak to me before Mass," she said: "I want to keep thinking of Holy God." At midnight she was carried to the church. The First Mass had already been said, and now the second had begun. It was a scene of prayer, love and adoration.

There, in her accustomed place before the Sanctuary, was Nellie. Her pallid, wasted face foretold that this was to be her last Christmas on earth, yet it was radiant with holiness and love—for was she not to receive her Holy God on this, the night He first came down to dwell among His children? Now her head was bowed in prayer, now she raised her eyes and followed each movement and each gesture of God's minister.

Finally, the Sanctuary gates are opened wide and Jesus of Bethlehem comes to little Nellie to give her His Christmas gift—His Eucharist—His own dear Self.

Nellie's face, before so pale and haggard, was glowing now; her eyes were bright with some strange brilliance, staring fixidly at the Tabernacle as if they penetrated the secrets of His hidden life. "If ever anyone was in ecstasy," declared Sister Mary of St. Pius, who had knelt next to the child, "Nellie certainly was then."

Back in her bed, Nellie could not rest, and she called Nurse. "Today is Holy God's Birthday, the day He came on earth to save us from sin, so light the candles, Mudder, please." When the crib was lighted up, Nellie's joy found vent in tears. When calmed, she sang several hymns.

Chapter 16

Growth in Virtue

THE seeds of virtue had been sown in little Nellie's heart by a holy Irish mother, they had been nurtured by the teaching and example of the pious Sisters. Then God Himself had come, and, warmed by the sunshine of His presence and bedewed by the waters of His grace, they blossomed forth, producing abundant fruit. Patience, humility, obedience, kindness, a purity that was angelic and a sublime trust in Divine Providence radiated from Nellie's every word and action.

Nellie endured her long and painful illness with extraordinary patience. "Her fortitude in suffering was heroic," wrote His Lordship the Bishop of Cork. "She was afflicted with many maladies, among them caries of the jawbone. The wound had to be treated with disinfectants every day, which caused the child intense pain. She endured the agony without a complaint or even an exclamation, always clasping the crucifix tightly in her little hands."

The little sufferer sought no human sympathy. "Holy God suffered far more on de Cross for me," she said. Not that she did not experience the struggle when fallen nature combats grace, and bodily suffering makes even the holiest souls irritable and impatient. One day Reverend Mother showed her something; with a gesture of impatience, Nellie bade her go away. Later on, however, she called for Mother and would not be content until she came. "Mudder, forgib' me, I won't do it any more," she said between her sobs; and throwing her arms around Mother's neck, she embraced her tenderly. During the remainder of that day her oft-repeated acts of sorrow and the sad expression of her childish countenance told clearly how she repented that word and gesture of impatience.

Nellie frequently humbled herself before God and asked Him to pardon her sins and imperfections. One day Mother Magdalen was holding the little patient in her arms, and, thinking that Nellie had fallen asleep, she said to Nurse: "How happy this child is! She will go straight to Heaven, for she never committed a sin." Nellie started, raised her head and said, sadly and humbly, "Oh, yes, Mudder, I did; I told a lie once."

Nellie's trust in Divine Providence was most remarkable. This world belonged to Holy God, and nothing happened that was not His Will. One day, Sister Mary of St. Francis de Sales said to her, "Baby, when you go to Holy God, tell Him Mother Francis wants some money to pay her debts." Nellie replied simply, "Holy God knows it, and dat's enough."

The New Year 1908 dawned, but it brought no earthly hope to those who loved little Nellie. It was a wonder to all how she continued to exist: the tiny frame was quite exhausted. She could now retain nothing, not even a spoonful of broth. She seemed to live on the Blessed Sacrament alone. Her sufferings were so great that one day they drew tears from a Sister who witnessed them. But Nellie was quite resigned. "Why are you crying, Mudder?" she asked. "You should be glad dat I am going to Holy God." If Nurse complained of a headache or other pain, Nellie would say, "What is that compared to what Holy God suffered for us."

On another occasion one of the nuns went to Nellie and begged her to pray for a sister of hers, a lady in the world, who was very ill.

"Has she children, Mudder?" asked this astounding infant.

"She has many children," replied the Good Shepherd Sister, quite gravely.

"Then," said Nellie confidently, "I will pray to Holy God, and He will see that she'll be cured." And, in fact, the lady recovered.

Sister M. Immaculata once stayed up late until

4 a.m. illuminating an address for the Countess of Aberdeen and therefore overslept for Mass. She came up hoping to receive Holy Communion with Nellie, but Nellie was too ill that morning. Nellie heard Sister say, "I have missed my Communion." Much as she loved Sister Immaculata, Nellie would not speak to her for two days, saying: "She did not get up to receive Holy God. If Mudder had been ill—but only sleepy!" Two days later, putting her loving arms around her neck, Nellie said: "Mudder, I forgive you." To the same Sister when she was ill, Nellie said, "Holy God will cure you and make you strong, for you have a good deal of work to do for Him"—and the Sister, who had been frail, became strong. To Sister Immaculata Nellie also said: "When I shall be with Holy God, you take this," showing her a Scapular of the Sacred Heart and a Rosary of the Immaculate Conception. "These will make you better and stronger." Sister carried them always.

Nellie liked medals and holy pictures and had them arranged around her bed. She would call attention to them, telling others to look at this or that, as she named her heavenly friends. Noticing that Sister Teresa had a nice medal on her rosary, Nellie asked, "Have you one for me?"

Nellie had been asked to pray for the recovery of two Sisters who were invalids. Of one, Nellie said that Holy God would cure her because she had a lot of work to do for Him; of the other, she said that Holy God would make her better, but He would not cure her. These predictions were fully realized.

Shortly after Christmas, Nellie had been enrolled in the Apostleship of Prayer. The meaning of the Association had been explained to her; she seemed to grasp it fully, and she redoubled her prayers for the Pope—"*my own* Holy Fadder," she called him—and for "my bishop," for the needs of the Church and for sinners, those who pain Holy God. She prayed for the Souls in Purgatory and for her own "dead mother."

On one occasion, Sister Immaculata had begged—almost commanded—Nellie to offer her Communion on a certain morning for the nurse's brother. Nellie became agitated. She could not do that, she said, and she was greatly troubled. Finally driven to an explanation by their comments, she told them, half crying, "Holy God says I must offer it for my Holy Fadder!"*

On the occasion of Nellie's enrollment in the Apostleship of Prayer, Reverend Mother showed her a picture of the Sacred Heart. The child examined it closely and responded, "Dat is not de way I saw Holy God."

---

* Another source recounts the same incident, or a very similar one, in which Nellie states that Holy God says she must give her Communion to Mother Francis.

"How did you see Him?" asked Mother.

"Dis way," answered Nellie, holding her hands on her breast in the same manner as on the occasion when she had spoken of her vision to Sister Immaculata and Nurse Hall. Mother was astonished; she had not heard of this "visit of Holy God" before. She spoke to the Sister and the Nurse, and they gave thanks to God. Their lips were opened now, and they disclosed their treasured secret.

∼ *Chapter 17* ∼

Last Days on Earth

NELLIE'S silent communings with God became daily longer and more frequent. She often asked others to leave her room, as she wished to speak to Holy God. Sometimes they asked her if she were not lonely or afraid during their absence, but the answer was always the same: "Oh, no! I was talkin' to Holy God." If they questioned her further, she would answer: "Holy God says I muss not speak of dese tings."

Nellie had been asked to pray for the recovery of a well-known Jesuit Father who was unable to come to Cork because of a serious illness. "Holy God is very fond of Fadder _____," she said a few days later. "He will get better, but he will never see me." Her words proved true.

During the month of January the little patient lingered on, enduring her sufferings with heroic fortitude. Fr. Scannell says that "days of torture glided into weeks of agony, till sympathetic hearts would pray that God might take her."

Nellie was told that the more patiently she bore

her sufferings, the nearer she would hereafter be to Holy God. "But Mudder," said Nellie, "I will fly to Him."

Nellie said that she would go to Holy God on His own day (Sunday); that she would wear her First Communion dress, that she would go in Nurse's arms, and that they should make a new dress for Nurse.

Her strength was failing day by day; the end was close at hand. On Thursday, the 30th of January, Mother Francis came to see her. Knowing that the child's life was nearly spent, she spoke of what was dearest to her heart. "Nellie," she said, "when you go to Holy God, will you ask Him to take me to Him? I am longing for Heaven." The child looked searchingly at Mother, and her wonderful eyes seemed to glow with some preternatural light. Then she answered solemnly: "Holy God can't take you, Mudder, till you are better and do what He wants you to do."*

On that same day Nellie sang several little hymns; then, calling Nurse, she said to her:

"Tell me, Mudder, how do you feel today?"

"Very well, Nellie," answered Nurse.

"But tell me," continued Nellie, "do you feel you are nearing Holy God? I do."

"All who visited Little Nellie were struck by her

---

* Mother Francis lived to be 99 years old. She died in 1960 at the Good Shepherd Home in St. Paul, Minnesota.

extraordinary sanctity," says Fr. Scannell. "In the presence of that child, they felt that they stood on the confines of the supernatural."

One day the confessor of the community, a holy Capuchin Father named Pere Fidele,* went in to see her. The priest impressed Nellie very much, and when he rose to take his leave, she asked him for his blessing. Father Fidele, who had been amazed by Nellie's very evident growth in holiness, said to her quite sincerely: "Child, it is not I who should bless you; it is you who must bless me"—and with true Franciscan simplicity he bent knee and head before her. Nellie obeyed with equal simplicity. She took the holy water font and, moistening her finger, made the Sign of the Cross on his forehead, saying, "God bless you, Fadder," very fervently. Ever afterward she gave her child-like blessing in like manner to all who asked for it.

One day, however, she did it differently, and that was the very day before her death. A lady of high social standing from Queenstown (now called Cobb) had begged to be permitted to see Nellie. The Reverend Mother was unwilling to disturb the child, who was evidently in her last hours, but the lady had her way. She was experiencing dreadful spiritual anguish and could find no relief for her troubled soul. She hoped this

---

* According to Margaret Gibbons, this priest was the "Tarcisius" of the *Father Matthew Record,* October, 1911.

saintly child might help her. The lady drew near the bed. Nellie fixed her great eyes on the world-weary face before her. Though Nellie was so weak as to be scarcely able to move her hand, her forceful will prevailed. She just managed to dip her finger in the holy water, and she painfully traced the Sign of the Cross on the lady's forehead with the usual formula, "God bless you"—but in this one instance she added, *"and comfort you."*

As Nellie had never used those words before, all were surprised. But upon leaving, the lady told the prioress that after those words were spoken, her interior anguish disappeared and her soul became filled with a wonderful peace. The next day, the lady sent as a token of her gratitude a fragrant bunch of greenhouse violets. They were laid in the dead child's folded hands.

A couple of days before Nellie's death, Mother Superior had asked her: "Nellie, what will you ask Holy God for me when you see Him?" Nellie answered at once: "Dat He may lob you berry much and dat you may do much good."

"Rosary tickets" for the month of February were distributed by lot among the children, and Nellie in her turn drew hers. It proved to be that of the Feast of the Purification, February 2, which was to fall on the upcoming Sunday. Would that be the day? On Friday Nellie was so weak that it was thought she had already passed away, but again she rallied slightly. She passed an agonizing night. On Saturday the little sufferer hung between life and death.

All day on February 2, poor little Nellie's agony was heartrending to behold. Several Sisters came in turn to kneel in prayer around the little bed; three remained, becoming witnesses of Nellie's saintly death.

Toward three o'clock Nellie became quite calm, and she remained motionless for about an hour. Her eyes were fixed on something which she seemed to see at the foot of her bed. "There was an extraordinary look in those lovely eyes," a Sister related; "it was not the sightless, glazed expression of the dying." Then Nellie moved. Her eyes now filled with tears—with tears of joy, it seemed. She tried to rise and draw near to that "something" on which she was gazing so longingly, and then she smiled. From the movement of her lips it seemed she was speaking with someone, and raising her eyes, she followed with a look of supernatural love that "something," which seemed now to hover above her head. Presently, with an ecstatic smile, little Nellie "flew" to Holy God. It was four o'clock on Sunday, February 2, 1908, the Feast of the Purification of Mary and of the Presentation of the Child Jesus in the Temple (Candlemas Day). Nellie was then four years, five months and eight days old.

∽ Chapter 18 ∽

Little Nellie of Holy God

NELLIE'S body was laid out on the bed which had been her cross, clothed in her First Communion dress and wearing the wreath and veil and her dainty little shoes. Around the bed were placed the pictures, medals and other objects of piety which she had loved so much in life; all these became precious relics.

In the morning, the little coffin was carried to the chapel and laid in the children's choir. Then, after the Requiem Mass, the Sisters and the pupils came to bid a last farewell. They touched the little hand with rosaries and medals and reverently kissed the body that had housed a soul so dear to God.

In the evening the little cortege wended its way almost unnoticed in those busy, bustling streets to the public cemetery across the Valley of the Lee. Nellie's remains were confined to consecrated ground in St. Joseph's Cemetery. The mourners were few: Nellie's sister Mary, who was still a pupil at St. Finbarr's School; Nurse Hall; Sister

Teresa (a Tourière); and some of the pupils.

All who had known little Nellie intimately in life believed that she was now a saint of God. They felt she did not need their prayers; they rather prayed to her to intercede for them with God.

As the story of the remarkable life of that holy child spread among the public, the little grave in St. Joseph's Cemetery gradually became a shrine. The graces obtained through her intercession were by degrees divulged, and the resting place of this little child became celebrated throughout the country.

Nellie's Body Found Intact

It was now sought to have the remains transferred to the Convent Cemetery at Sunday's Well. Exactly a year and a week after little Nellie's death, the grave was opened to see if such transference could with safety be accomplished.

The Reverend Dr. Scannell will now tell us what took place at the exhumation:

"There were present a well-known priest [this was Fr. Scannell himself], the Nurse, and two other reliable witnesses. To the great astonishment of all (for it must be borne in mind that the child had died of phthisis*), the body was found

---

* phthisis (pronounced: thī sis)—a wasting or consumption of the tissue; usually, pulmonary tuberculosis.

intact, except for a small cavity in the right jaw which corresponded to the bone that had been destroyed by caries whilst the little one was still alive. The fingers were quite flexible and the hair had grown a little. The dress, the wreath and veil of First Communion, with which she had been buried as she desired, were still intact. The silver medal of the saintly child of Mary was bright as if it had been recently polished; everything, in fact, was found to be exactly as on the day of Nellie's death."

The permission of the authorities, civil and ecclesiastical, having been obtained, the body was transferred from the public cemetery to that of the Good Shepherd Convent, where it was piously laid on the 8th of September, 1909. It was a gloomy day with clouded sky, yet scarcely had the interment begun when the sun burst through the clouds that had shrouded it; and from some distant tower a clear-toned bell kept tolling sweetly as the last sods fell upon the grave of "Little Nellie of Holy God."

Father Scannell reports, "The (new) grave is visited by groups of pious persons who ask that little Nellie may plead for them before the throne of the All-powerful God. The blind, the deaf, the lame, those in suffering or in sorrow, seek health and comfort at this peaceful holy shrine."

Nor did they seek in vain. A photo published as

late as 1924* shows the grave strewn with crutches and medical boots. These tokens of the power of the child's intercession were removed for reasons of prudence in 1929.

The *Father Matthew Record* of October 11, 1911 had noted: "Many favors obtained after recourse had been had to Nellie's aid are related. . . . Scarcely a day passes that notification of some such case does not reach the Sisters of the School of St. Finbarr."

Little Nellie as Intercessor

Mother Mary of St. Francis Xavier, Superior of the Convent of the Good Shepherd at Sunday's Well during Nellie's lifetime, has left the following testimony regarding Nellie as intercessor during her short life and after her death:

"One afternoon as I returned from Vespers I stopped in the infirmary to see Nellie. As I made ready to leave, Nellie urged me to stay and talk to her. "O, Baby, I can't," I said. "I must go and tidy my desk. I have mislaid a letter and must look for it." "Never mind, Mudder," she assured me, "I'll find all your things for you." She has kept her word. Never have I lost anything that she has not found for me. Sometimes she likes to tease, playfully keeping me

---

* See *Little Nellie of Holy God,* by Rev. J. Carr, C.SS.R., 1924, Gill & Sons.

searching, but not for long. I heartily recommend our readers to have recourse with confidence to Nellie for the recovery of lost articles.

"Not the least of her roles as intercessor in Heaven is her predilection for expectant mothers. Scarcely was her little heart stilled in death when she began to show her power with God in this regard. One of our Sisters had a married sister who was expecting a baby very soon. All her babies so far (this was the fourth) had been stillborn. The relatives were inconsolable, for the attending physician feared not only for the safety of the baby, but even for the life of the mother. Our Sisters besought Nellie to intercede with Holy God in behalf of both the mother and the child. She did not keep them long waiting. Nellie died at four o'clock Sunday afternoon; at four o'clock the next morning a beautiful, robust baby was born.

"Numberless similar cases could be cited. A novena of one Our Father and nine Hail Marys in honor of the nine months our Blessed Mother carried the Divine Infant in her most pure womb, with an additional Our Father and Hail Mary in thanksgiving for the graces bestowed on Little Nellie during her short life, has brought many similar favors since her death.

"May God be forever adored, blessed, and praised for the marvels His grace has wrought in the soul of this little one. And may Little Nellie from her place of repose in the Bosom of the Eternal Father look down with compassion on all of us still striving in this land of exile and obtain for us all the graces necessary to keep our hearts, like hers, so innocent and pure that when the journey ends we may literally 'fly up to Holy God.'"

Pope St. Pius X Asks for a Relic
Of Little Nellie

If, during her lifetime, Bishop O'Callaghan showed himself a devoted friend to Nellie, after her death he was no less so. When Pope St. Pius X, impressed by the facts related to him of Nellie's life, asked for a relic, Bishop O'Callaghan was extremely pleased. His sister relates the circumstances connected with its presentation:

"My brother showed great satisfaction at the Pope's request for a relic and cast about to find something that might serve as a case in which to send it. He bethought himself of a valuable gold locket of large size, a family heirloom in my possession. 'Would I give it,' he asked. I willingly assented. The locket was altered to suit its present requirements; my brother had a delicately chased monstrance with a Host engraved upon it. The relic was then laced within the locket and forwarded to Rome, where it was received by His

Holiness with great devotion."*

Madame Merry del Val, mother of His Eminence Cardinal Merry del Val, Vatican Secretary of State under Pope Pius X, likewise begged Bishop O'Callaghan for a relic, which was later on presented by the Countess to the Queen of Spain.

The Bishop lost no time in opening a Court of Enquiry concerning Nellie's virtues, this being the first step toward possible canonization. He was not destined, however, to see his hopes realized. Pope St. Pius X died in August 1914 and he himself did in 1916. God's time evidently had not yet come. May Nellie herself from her fair heavenly home hasten it.

Postscript

After 1914-1918, Nellie's father, Mr. William Organ, returned to his native Waterford and was employed as sacristan in one of the local churches. Leo Madigan (see p. xii) relates that William remarried and had two more children, Kitty and Stephen. William Organ was highly

---

* "Pope Pius X asked him [Bishop O'Callaghan] for a relic of Little Nellie, so he sent him a piece of her hair which was cut off when her body was exhumed. All his correspondence was translated and presented to the Pope by Don Ugo Descuffi." —From a letter of Sister Imelda O'Driscoll, Good Shepherd Sisters, Sunday's Well, to the editor of TAN Books and Publishers, Inc., December 30, 1991.

respected, and it is said that upon his death at age 72, on a Christmas Day, the people of Waterford turned out in the thousands to pay their respects to this man who had endeared himself to his people. According to Mr. Madigan, many of the descendants of William Organ's second family live in Dungarvan.

Little Nellie's two brothers, Thomas and David, and her sister Mary went to England after completing their education. One boy joined the merchant navy, the other the army. Mary became a seamstress and did the sewing for the boys in the Jesuit College in England until she married Mr. Evans. She had three children—two girls and a boy.

Nellie Organ is among the "Persons in Waterford History" who are featured on the website of Waterford County Museum.

On December 8, 1984, a plaque to honor Little Nellie of Holy God, the "Little Violet of the Holy Eucharist," was erected on the exterior wall of the parish church ("Ballybricken Church") in Portlaw, County Waterford. Crowds of parishioners and people from neighboring counties were present at the ceremony, which took place after the celebration of Holy Mass by His Lordship Michael Russell, who was then Bishop of Waterford and Lismore.

The following information comes from a letter of Sister Imelda O'Driscoll, R.G.S., of the Good Shepherd Sisters, Sunday's Well, Cork, Ireland, written to the present publishers in 1991:

"Nellie's sister, Mary, died on the 15th of September, 1990, at the ripe old age of 91. Her ashes are buried near Nellie in our cemetery. Nellie's family died in England; her nieces and nephews are over there. Her father fought in France during the 1914-1918 war [World War I]; he retired in Waterford and spent the remainder of his life as sacristan in one of the churches there. Like his daughter he died on a Sunday, also a very holy death. . . . Nellie's mother is buried in Spike Island."

∼ Appendix 1 ∼

The "Heavenly Light" at Nellie's First Communion

A PRIEST* wrote in October, 1911, describing Nellie's thanksgiving after her First Communion:

"The happy moment will long be remembered by those who had the privilege of being present. Nellie seemed in an ecstasy, and all remarked the heavenly light that lighted up the child's countenance."

And Reverend Dr. Scannell wrote: "Still she sat there motionless, insensible to things of earth, in silent, loving conference with the Saviour, her radiant countenance reflecting the Eternal Light within her."

The priest author of the article in the *Father Matthew Record* states that "this light gave her hair a rich, golden glow." The French author of

---

* "Tarcisius" in the *Father Matthew Record,* October, 1911. This same priest gave her Holy Communion on more than one occasion.

La Petite Violette, to make certain about this alleged light, asked the Mother Superior of the convent in Cork the following questions:

1. It is said in the first notice,* edited January 1911, in Rome, that at the moment of her First Communion, Nellie's face radiated as if suffused with a celestial light. Was this fact truly distinctive and quite above the ordinary, and should the expressions used in recounting it be taken literally?

2. In the same notice it is said again, speaking of the child's frequent Communions, that, after having received, *Nellie's countenance was transfigured.* Here again, one earnestly desires enlightenment. Had the child then a countenance more recollected, an attitude more impressing, or else did her face really radiate in an inexplicable manner, so much so that one remarked it and was astonished as at something unusual and altogether unheard of?

We copy with exactness the Reverend Mother's replies to the above, dated June 27, 1911.

1. "At the moment of her First Communion, which she received in a transport of love, Nellie's features shone as if the presence of the great Light within her reflected Itself in her face. Yes,

---

* This "notice" was a biographical sketch written by Don Ugo Descuffi from materials supplied him, toward the close of 1910, by the Most Reverend Dr. O'Callaghan, O.P., Bishop of Cork.

those who saw Nellie then are well convinced that the child's appearance was not at all ordinary. This phenomenon was seen more particularly at her other Communions, because after her first, she was taken almost immediately out of the chapel, and there were only a chosen few who had the happiness of witnessing the (wonder) *which really did take place.*

2. "No. Nellie had not only then a countenance more recollected, an attitude more pious. That she had always; but the *extraordinary radiance* which I cannot define, *but which I have seen,* astonished not only believers, but also the incredulous."

Appendix 2

Little Nellie and Pope St. Pius X

C ATHOLIC periodicals in Europe had made their readers acquainted with the leading facts of Nellie's brief life before the end of 1909. The decree *Quam Singulari,* by which Pope Pius X admitted and exhorted to Holy Communion children of the tenderest years, was promulgated in August, 1910. The claim that there was a strictly historical connection between Nellie and *Quam Singulari* is supported by two recorded facts. These are as follows:

1. The *Father Matthew Record* of December, 1911, quoting from the May, 1911 edition of *Roma,* published in Rome, reads: "Yesterday the Holy Father gave an audience with a little history attached to it to two ladies, Signorina Caymari, Mrs. FitzGerald and a little girl." (Here follows an account of the zealous good works inaugurated and carried on by the Signorina, especially that of preparing children for their First Communion.)

Then: "Among the last batch of expectant First Communicants was one little girl who seemed doomed never to approach the Holy Table, for in the midst of her preparations she was seized with meningitis; other complications ensued and the doctor declared that she must inevitably die. Then someone proposed that all the children should petition Little Nellie, the Irish child about whom our readers were informed *a few years ago* [italics added] to secure this great grace for their comrade. To the astonishment of the doctors the girl recovered, with the result that she was presented yesterday to the Holy Father, who listened with great interest to the touching story." The few years previous to 1911 bring us back again to the French sketch supplied by Mr. O'Malley-Moore in 1909, and edited by the Belgian priest.* *Roma* would, of course, copy and comment on the then most unusual circumstance of an infant First Communicant, with all its attendant significances; this conjecture is practically confirmed by recorded fact 2, which I [Margaret Gibbons] heard from the Reverend Mother's own lips.

2. A Monsignor from Rome was visiting the Convent of Sunday's Well when Mother Francis Xavier was Superior there. He assured the nuns there that long before the composition of his

---

* Cf. Gibbons (see p. ix of the present book), p. 2.

decree *Quam Singulari,* Pope Pius X had heard of
Nellie's longing for and admission to Sacramental
union with Our Lord. Some casual official of the
Vatican, the Monsignor said, brought the facts to
the notice of Pope Pius X, and he, on reading
them, turned eagerly to his Cardinal Secretary
and cried: "There! That is the sign for which I was
waiting." Before the close of 1910 the famous
decree encouraging early Communion was promulgated.

From the day of Nellie's exhumation, prayer
had been made without ceasing by the children of
Sunday's Well that Nellie might work a "big mir-
acle" (their own phrase) which would obtain for
her little companions, and all little children, the
great favor of receiving Holy Communion as
nearly as possible to the age at which she had
received—rather than at the age of ten or twelve,
according to the custom then current.

When the decree of Pope Pius X, *Quam singu-
lari,* was published in August, 1910, the girls at
St. Finbarr's were confident that their prayers
had brought it into being. They wrote thanking
His Holiness, and at the same time begged the
Pope to canonize their little classmate and make
her the Patroness of early First Communicants.
The Holy Father's reply to this letter [See Appen-
dix 3] was published in Father Scannell's life of
Little Nellie, which came out about this time.

The longest biography of Little Nellie is a French one by Père des Roncés. In that biography* are found the approbations of no less than eight Cardinals and forty-four Archbishops and Bishops, including Cardinal Bourne, Cardinal Vannutelli and Cardinal Mercier.

The story of the presenting of a copy of Père des Roncés' biography to the Pope by Abbé Prevost is worth relating. Scarcely had Pope Pius X heard the child's name pronounced than his features, ordinarily so sad, lighted up with a kindly smile.

"Oh!" he exclaimed, "so they want me to canonize her . . . but that is unheard of in the Church, a child of four! . . . We have, it is true, a little Saint of two-and-a-half years, but that is a martyr, St. Simon of Trente. In the case of martyrs it is easier."

"Nevertheless, Holy Father," replied the Abbé, "it is certain that little Nellie practiced virtue in an heroic degree, and Your Holiness would be convinced of it if you would deign to read what is set forth in these pages."

"Yes," said the Pope, "she was a little angel, her patience was admirable, her resignation in suffering perfect. Moreover, she showed a superior intelligence in supernatural matters. As for her

---

* Bernard des Roncés, *Nellie, la petite violette du saint-sacrement, morte en odeur de sainteté, le 2 Février 1908, à lâge de 4 ans et 5 mois.* Paris: Maison du Bonpasteur, 1912.

innocence, it is beyond a doubt . . . she was an angel, living with angels."

Abbé Prevost then mentioned the many favors from all quarters of the globe that had been attributed to Nellie's intercession. The Holy Father was sympathetic, but he responded, "God must manifest His Will by miracles."* Then, taking up the richly bound volume of her life, he added playfully, "From a little life, you have made a big book."

Turning over the leaves, the Pope came across Nellie's photograph. "Ah, there she is!" he exclaimed, gazing at it benevolently.

At the close of the audience, Abbé Prevost presented a copy of Perè des Roncés' book with these words:

"Most Holy Father, humbly prostrate at the feet of Your Holiness, I venture to beg your acceptance of this life of Little Nellie, the Little Violet of the Blessed Sacrament.

"This angelic child of but four years is an attractive model of virtue to all little children, especially by her love for the Holy Eucharist, and her ardent desire to receive it. Her clients have been pleased, with reason, to call her the angelic forerunner of the Decree *Quam Singulari*. It appears to us that one of the most practical and

---

* Another source gives the Holy Father's response as, "That is well. She must obtain miracles."

efficacious means of a faithful correspondence to the saving Decree would be the spreading abroad of this life. Priests and educators of youth find therein a powerful aid to their ministry, as numerous witnesses bear testimony.

"Deign, Your Holiness, to bless our efforts, and those of the priests and the 'Leaguers' [members of the Irish Crusaders League] who second us by their devoted help."

Pope Pius X took up his pen and wrote:

"May God enrich with every blessing Abbé Prevost and all those who recommend frequent Communion to little boys and girls, proposing Nellie as their model.

Pope Pius X. June 4th, 1912

Letter of Pope St. Pius X

Autograph Reply Addressed to the Children of
St. Finbarr's School by His Holiness Pope Pius X
(Official Translation).

TO THE beloved children of the School of the Sisters of the Good Shepherd in Cork, with sincerest congratulations on the sentiments expressed in their pious address of true love for Our Lord Jesus Christ in the Most Holy Sacrament of the Eucharist, with the warmest thanks for their prayers for the Holy Catholic Church and for Us, and with the wish that they may always keep as good as their companion, Nellie, who was called to Heaven while still a little child, where she is praying for them, for the comfort of their families, for the Sisters their dear mistresses, for their superiors, and especially for their very venerable Bishop, to all of whom We earnestly impart the Apostolic Blessing.

The Vatican, November 24, 1910
Pius P. P. X

Article on Little Nellie from *The Catholic Encyclopedia*

From Supplement I, Volume XVII, published by
The Gilmary Society, New York, 1922, p. 563.

Organ, NELLIE, better known as LITTLE NELLIE
OF HOLY GOD, b. in Waterford, Ireland, 24 August,
1903; d. there 2 February, 1908. This saintly child
was the daughter of humble Catholic parents
whose only inheritance was a sterling Irish faith.
The youngest of four children, Nellie was not four
years old when her mother died and she, with her
sister, was placed in the Industrial School of the
Sisters of the Good Shepherd, at Sunday's Well in
1907. It was soon discovered that she was suffering from phthisis and curvature of the spine. As
her frail little body wasted away, her heart and
soul opened to the love of God and the illumina-
tion of His grace in an extraordinary degree. She
had a wonderful intuition concerning the Real
Presence, and her progress in religious knowledge and growth in holiness were most remarkable. She lived continuously in the presence of

"Holy God," and her hunger to receive Him in Holy Communion was so great that the Bishop of Cork permitted her to make her First Communion, a permission more unusual then, before the promulgation of the decree of Pope Pius X in favor of early Communion, than now. During the remaining months of her life, her patience in suffering for the love of "Holy God," many extraordinary spiritual facts attested by the Sisters who witnessed them, the hours she spent in "talking to Holy God," and the secrets He revealed to her convinced those who came in contact with her of her unusual sanctity. She was buried in the public cemetery of St. Joseph where her grave became a shrine, at which, it was rumored, many found peace and consolation. A year and a half after her death, her body was transferred to the Convent Cemetery at Sunday's Well. At the disinterment her remains were found to be intact, the fingers quite flexible, and her clothing exactly as it was on the day of her death.

EDITH DONOVAN.

Little Nellie of Holy God

To Little Nellie of Holy God
  This little song I sing:
A babe of four years old, or odd,
  A frail afflicted thing,
Within whose soul baptismal grace
  Was with such heavenly wisdom wed,
That in the Sacramental Bread
  She saw God clearly face to face.

From her fifth year of Hallowed Bread
  The blessed child partook;
Then lying silent on her bed
  Throughout the day would brook
No food, no mirth, no play.
  "What are you doing, little Nell?"
The Sister asked, who loved her well—
  "Talking to Holy God," she'd say.

Full thirty times Christ's Flesh and Blood
  Made glad this sinless child;
Then as the snowdrops were in bud,
  Like them all undefiled,

97

Her blue eyes opened on a Sun
    That knows no setting. Holy God,
Who walks in paths by sin untrod,
    Had found in Nellie such a one.

She died. And then they buried her
    Where all the town are laid,
But in the fall the following year
    They brought the little maid
Back to a convent grave, and then
    No blight of death on her was found,
Aglow her cheeks, her flesh all sound,
    A joy to angels and to men.

"Let little children come to Me,
    And scare them not away."
So said the Lord in Galilee,
    So will He ever say;
Then, be you one who would have part
    With Him in never ending bliss,
Take heed this sign you do not miss,
    How God doth love the clean of heart.

                                        C. W. Farraud, S.J.

Prayer

O JESUS, Divine Friend of little children, we thank Thee for the signal graces Thou didst confer upon Thy holy servant, Little Nellie, by inspiring her with such great devotion to Thy Sacred Passion and such ardent love of Thy Blessed Eucharist.

Grant, we beseech Thee, O Lord, the fulfillment of Thy designs regarding Thy loving little servant, for Thy greater glory and for the sanctification of souls.

We adore Thee, O Jesus, ever present in the Blessed Sacrament; we pray that Thy Sacred Presence may be honored daily more and more; that the little ones, whom Thou desirest to come to Thee, may frequently approach Thy Holy Table.

O Sacrament Most Holy, O Sacrament Divine,
all praise and all thanksgiving
be every moment Thine.

Imprimatur
✠ T. A. O'Callaghan, O.P.
Bishop of Cork